D1187236

Life and Love and Everything

This book is dedicated to the children of:

Byron Court Primary School, Wembley
Catton Grove Middle School, Norwich
Lyon Park Junior School, Wembley
St Anselm's School, Harrow

Life and Love and Everything

Children's Questions Answered by Claire Rayner

Kyle Cathie Limited

Introduction

I've been answering people's questions for a very long time. Twelve years of nursing started me out on my task as an information giver; thirty years of running newspaper and magazine problem pages consolidated it.

During these years, I received a steady trickle of letters asking me for help and information from young – very young – people. Indeed as soon as they could write, it seemed, some of them chose to write to an outsider for answers to important questions that worried them.

The more such letters I received, the more certain I became that there were lots more children who had questions they might like to ask someone like me, but weren't sure how to make contact; so I asked teacher friends at a few schools what they thought.

They agreed with me. They asked the young people they were teaching if they'd like to send me questions, and indeed they did! In large numbers. I could only include a small selection of them in this little book, which is the result of my conversations with those teachers. Every one of these letters was written by a child of primary school age (under eleven) who decided for him or herself to ask it. Their teachers gave them the opportunity to write to me but did not suggest the questions. If they had perhaps some of them wouldn't have been quite so difficult. Like "Why am I alive?" . . .

I've done my best to answer them honestly and not only with my opinions. I've spent a lot of time checking that I'd got facts right – because I certainly don't know all the answers to life and love and everything. However, I do know how to find out and that was what I set out to do for my young correspondents.

I hope you, whether you're an adult or a child, find these questions and answers interesting. I think the questions are fascinating, and certainly give lie to the belief held by far too many people that children don't think deeply. They do, and are capable of expressing their thoughts clearly and succinctly and with great honesty.

If this small collection does nothing more than convince readers that children may be less informed than adults but that certainly does not mean they're stupid or lacking in thoughtfulness, then it will more than justify its publication. In fact, many of these letters make it clear to me, at any rate, that they're a good deal more thoughtful than many adults. A fact which cheers me greatly when I think about the future. I hope you'll be cheered too.

Dear Steven,

There is no answer to your question, except that – well you just are! In any family where there is more than one child, someone has to be the second or third or whatever. The order in which particular people arrive is a total accident. It just wasn't possible for your Mum and Dad to sit down together one day and say, "I know! Let's make a baby. And let's make Steven first. After that, we'll make his brother." They just had to wait and see who turned up when their babies were born.

It's not a bad thing to be the youngest, is it? It doesn't mean you're any less important than your big brother. You just happen to be Steven who was born after him.

Maybe you won't always be the youngest. Maybe one day your Mum and Dad will make another baby, and you'll be able to answer that baby's question about why he or she is the youngest, when they're old enough to ask. And you'll have to say, just as I say to you, "There is no answer to your question . . ."

Dear Clare Rayner

I was wondering if you

~~will~~

could answer my question for me please.

Why am I the second son born in my family

yours Sincerely

Steven

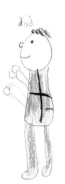

Dear Cheron,

Not all grown-ups think children need pocket money. They say, "Oh, tell me what you want, and I'll get it for you." Or they say, "Children don't need money. They only waste it."

Other grown-ups think pocket money is a good idea. It makes children get used to the price of things (if someone else does all the shopping you never do find out, do you?) and it teaches them to understand how to use money carefully so that it lasts a whole week.

Have you asked your Mum and Dad why they don't give you pocket money? Perhaps they never thought about how it can be a way of helping you to learn.

And have you ever asked your Mum and Dad if you could earn some instead of just being given it? Maybe you could do extra jobs at home (as well as the ones like helping with the dishes and tidying up, which all children should do for nothing!), such as extra weeding in the garden or sweeping up leaves in the autumn?

I hope asking these questions helps you get your pocket money. When you get some, will you save as well as spend? It's quite a good thing to do.

Dear miss claire Rayner

I never get my

pocter money

and I am a

Cheron

Dear Clare Rayner,

How come some people that are older than others are sometimes smaller than others?

Why do animals have different noises?

Thankyou Yours Sincerely Aoifa

Dear Aoifa,

Your questions are very sensible ones. I used to wonder about these things too.

The reason some younger people are bigger than some older people is that we are all completely different from each other. If you look at the answer to the question Michael asks near the end of this book, you'll see I explain how we all inherit different things from our parents and grandparents and great-grandparents who came before them. The height we have is one of the things we inherit. Some people are born to be small and some are born to be tall, and the differences in their inheritance will show when they are quite young.

It's a good thing there are people of different heights, by the way. Some jobs can only be done by small people – jockeys who ride horses in races have to be small and light – and some have to be done by tall, heavy people – policemen and soldiers on guard duty have to be tall. Ballerinas have to be small and clothes models have to be tall.

The reason for animals making different noises is also partly due to inheritance. Just like us, animals inherit from their parents and ancestors the shapes of their mouths and the sorts of voices they have and that is why they make the same sorts of sound as they did. But there is another reason why animals' ancestors developed these sorts of mouths and voice boxes in the first place. They use sounds to signal to each other, often in places where they can't easily see each other.

It wouldn't be much use if a mother bird signalled to her baby bird that there was danger about if she sounded like every other mother bird in the whole world, would it? The baby bird wouldn't recognise her call. So, Nature has made it so that each species has its own special call sound, just as humans do.

However, within that particular call sound, there are differences of pitch (either high or low notes) and in some cases different languages, just like humans. Scientists have discovered that birds of the same species – say, sparrows – that are born in one part of Britain can't be understood by sparrows born in another part because they sing in a different "language". Isn't that interesting?

Dear Natalie,

I know hearing other people shouting at each other is horrid – it makes you feel all scared inside, doesn't it? – but anger isn't always a bad thing, you know. There are times when it is a very good thing to be angry and to let people know it.

For example, if you see a small child being hit and bullied by a big one, then that would make you angry (well, I hope it would! Everyone should get angry when they see that sort of unkindness and unfairness). Well, suppose you told the bully to stop and they didn't. You'd feel angry then, and it would be a very good thing for you to say very loudly how angry you were, even shouting it out. Then the bully would know you meant it, and might be scared enough to stop or even run away. And the small child would know you really cared about what happened, and feel a bit better.

Not all anger is for good reasons like that, of course. Sometimes people get angry because they're just feeling scratchy and miserable inside and want to get their bad feelings out and don't care who they shout at. (Have you never done that? I know I have!) Sometimes it's the bullies who get angry because they want their own way all the time and can't have it. There are as many reasons for getting angry as there are people, really. I hope you get angry when you see bad things happen and that you let the anger make you want to put the bad things right. If everyone did that, the world would be a much nicer place, I think.

Why do people get angry I
would like to know because
so meany people get angry.
I was walking home one-day
and I heard these two
people shouting and one
started to get angry so
the other one walked away.

Yours Sincerly
Natalie.

Dear Hellon,

All over your body, in your skin, there are tiny, tiny pockets called follicles. Inside each pocket is a root, a bit like a plant. Out of the root grows a single hair made of thousands and thousands of tiny building blocks called cells. The cells are added on at the bottom of each hair, and push the part that has already grown upwards and upwards all the time so that it sticks out of your skin. When the hair is very long it falls out, or maybe it gets pulled out or rubbed off, depending where it is on your skin. Then the root starts to grow another hair, pushing it up bit by bit till it comes out of the pocket and sticks out of your skin again.

In some places, like on your arms and legs and face, there aren't many follicles and the hairs are tiny and very soft. You can hardly see them, unless you look with a magnifying glass. In others, like your head, there are a lot more follicles, and they grow hair that is stronger and thicker, and you can see it easily. In some places, like the palms of your hands and the soles of your feet, there are no follicles at all. When you are older, some parts of your body, like under your arms and at the bottom of your belly, will start to get more follicles and grow more hairs which are thick.

So we aren't all that different from furry animals, are we?

Dear Claire,

How does your hair grow out of your head.

I hope you will write back. I Thank you for spending your time to read this letter.

Yours Sincerely
Hellon

Dear Rishi,

I am so sorry to hear how sad your family is because your Granddad died. But you know, it's right that everyone should be sad. He was a special person and everyone loved him and they miss him. If the family wasn't upset, it would mean that they hadn't loved him, wouldn't it?

So, in a way, it's a good thing the family is upset. It shows that everyone in it is a loving person who cares when someone is ill and dies and that should make you feel good. It would be miserable to have a family that didn't care at all.

It will get easier in your family as time goes by. Now, when people think about your Granddad, they can only think of their sad feelings that he isn't here any more. But soon they'll start to remember the funny things he said and the nice things he did and they'll smile when they think of him, instead of crying. At the end of a year from the time he died, most of the family will be like that, smiling more than crying. At the end of two years or so everyone will be smiling. It sounds a long time, but it won't be, not really. Just you wait and see!

my grand Dad died in
my family a month ago I
Real miss him a lot and he lived
with me It has made my
family upset

by Rishi

Dear Diana,

There was a time, long ago, when people believed that everything in the Bible actually happened.

Nowadays most people agree that though some of the things in the Bible might be true, quite a few of them are not. They are stories people invented thousands and thousands of years ago. The Adam and Eve story was invented to try to explain where people came from. Now we know, because of scientific investigations, that there was no need for there to be just one man and one woman ancestor for all the people in the world. We know that human beings developed from the tiny creatures that appeared in the gases and seas of the new planet, when Earth was first formed, right at the beginning of time, and are closely related to the animals, especially the monkeys and the apes and the chimpanzees. And that we appeared in lots of different places in the world, at different times.

So there never was an actual Adam and Eve, though it's a very attractive story, isn't it?

Dear Claire

How were our great Aunties and uncles boren beause Adam and Eve could not Be in all the Cuntries at the Same time?

Thank you
Yours sincerly.

Diurea

Dear Samantha,

What a very long letter you wrote! I hope when you grow up you decide to write stories because you write very interestingly.

Now, your problem. When people are still very young, the usual thing for them to do is to love someone, the way you loved Shaun when you were in the first grade, and then to stop loving them and to love someone else.

You're different in this matter of loving people and you're being rather grown up because your feelings of loving last so long. It seems to have been three whole years now that you've loved Shaun. Loving someone for a long time is what grown-ups do.

The trouble is, Shaun isn't as grown up as you are and is doing what most people of his and your age do, which is, well, going all over the place! One day he likes one girl, another day a different one. It isn't that he's bad, it's just that he's young.

All you can do, I think, is be patient and wait until your age catches up with your feelings. Maybe as the years go on passing, Shaun will come back to his first feelings for you and maybe your own feelings will last so long that one day you do indeed marry Shaun. It has happened to some people.

But don't count on it, Samantha. Most people grow up to marry quite different people from the ones they loved when they were very young. In the meantime, why not write some stories about people loving each other? I think you'd be very good at that and it could help you feel better about Shaun and Justine.

Dear
Jane Rainer,
When I was in the first grade I met this boy
Shaun. He is. very lovly and handsome. In the first
grade Shaun used to say to me do you love me
And I used to say the big yes! and he loved me
alot but when he found out that another boy Rodney
oved me he flew into a rage. He beat Rodney up
and gave him a black eye. Then the summer
holidays came up I thought oh no I woun't see
him for six weeks. After the summer holiday's
And I found out he didn't like me I thought of
the times when he wrote me love letters.
But I still loved him alot. Then came the time
when a girl named Zoe came along and she
beat me up. Shaun didn't say leave her alone
like he used to he said carry on beat her up.
Then six weeks went by I was missing
him more than ever. Now he hates me
Sometimes at wet-play we sit together
and talk about when we was in the
1st grade. He loves my freind Justina
I feel silly because he now goes
out with my freind.
what shall I do?
          Samantha

Dear Meena,

I think you've explained for yourself why your Mum keeps smacking you. It's because you don't listen to her.

Perhaps you can sit down with your Mum one day when she isn't cross with you for not listening and make a plan with her. Tell her that you will try always to listen to her in future. Tell her that you will try to do what she likes and that you will explain to her what goes wrong when you don't.

Then ask her if she will agree to stop smacking you.

This is called a deal. When you make a deal, you're supposed to keep to the arrangement very carefully. So, if you stop listening then your Mum will probably think she has to smack you again, but if you don't stop listening then she should keep her end of the deal and not smack you.

If she does and you don't think it's fair, is there anyone else in the family who can decide which of you is right? Perhaps your Dad or your Grandma could help.

Dear Clare Rayner,

I wonder if you can hlep me when my mum is all ways smacking me on my bottom because I dont listen to her and I hope you can hlep me on that.

Yours Faithfully
from meena patel

Dear Alex,

Nature is very clever. She never makes any animal do things it doesn't need to. She makes birds fast flyers because they need to catch fast-flying insects to eat and she makes tortoises slow because they eat leaves that don't run away from them when they come near.

There are two other reasons for animals being fast or slow. First of all, their weight. Tortoises aren't very big, but they are heavy because of their shells and heavy animals move slowly (think of elephants!). The other reason is to do with safety. If an animal might be caught and eaten by another one it has to be fast to get away (that's why mice are faster runners than cats) unless it has a good way of preventing itself from being eaten. And tortoises, remember, have their shells. It's hard to chew up a tortoise shell.

So that is why Herby moves slowly; but there is one time when he moves fast, of course. If something comes along that might hurt him, when he is walking about with his head and legs out of the shell, he moves his head and his four legs so fast, taking them into his shell to be safe, that you can barely see them go!

I hope you like this answer to your question.

PS Please give my regards to Herby.

Dear Claire

I would Like to know
Why Tortoises Move
Slowly.
I look forward to
hearing from you

Yours sincerely

Alex Bean.

This is My Tortoise Herby

Dear Nishma,

It is very nice when children are small, and they can get into bed with their Mum and Dad and all cuddle up together, though some parents' beds must get very crowded when there are three or four small children in a family.

It is a bit sad, of course, as children get older and there isn't room for them in their Mum and Dad's bed any more, but a lot of things change as you grow up. Some of them are for the better. It's lovely to be old enough to do things on your own. For example, when you were very small, you couldn't go out to play with your friends, and you do now, don't you? And you can stay up a bit later and join in grown-up family talk as you get older, instead of having to be put to bed very early.

But some of the changes are not for the better – like having to do things around the house to help (I hope you do!) and learning to be polite and to do as you are told, and, of course, not getting into bed with your parents. But there it is. Nobody can have everything, all the time.

All you can do now is go on going into your Mum and Dad's room to give them big cuddles and lots of them, but don't get into bed and crush them all up!

Dear claire Rayner
I keep on Jumping into
my mum's and dad's bed and
I get Squashed and so do my
Parents. Can you tell me
What to do.

Yours Sincerly

NishmA

Dear Stephanie,

I am so sorry your Mum and Dad are unhappy together and have decided not to live in the same house any more. It's very miserable for everyone when there is a divorce, though of course your Dad will still be your Dad, even if he isn't living with you. I hope good arrangements have been made for you to see him regularly.

The biggest trouble with divorce when there are children is if grown-ups don't tell the children all that is happening. They keep quiet not because they want to be unkind; quite the opposite, in fact. It's because they think talking about it all will worry children. Of course, what worries them most is what they don't understand and what they aren't told about.

I think this is why you are worrying about bedtimes and not wanting coffee. You want to go to bed earlier so that you can go to sleep and forget about your problems, and you get upset about silly little things like whether or not you want to drink coffee. It isn't the coffee that matters, is it? It's the divorce that is making you worry, and you aren't being told what's going on.

All you can do is tell your Mum (and Dad if possible) how upset you are, so that they can talk to you more and let you talk about how you feel. It won't make everything the way it used to be, of course, but it will help you to feel less sad and stop you from worrying so much.

I do hope things get better for you soon, Stephanie.

My name is Stephanie
and I go to bed at 9:00 I want to go
to bed at 8.00 wbbat Shal I Do
uD My Mum and Dad got Devost and I fel.
Sad

So what Shal I Do and I say that I
don't like Coffee But I have not trid it
So what shal I Do.

Stephanie

Dear Richard,

You've asked the most difficult question there is. Ever since people began to exist, millions of years ago, and looked at the world about them and began to think about what they saw, they've asked themselves this question about life.

So far, no one has come up with a complete answer.

There are people who will tell you that God made life and that is why we are alive. They are religious believers.

There are people who will tell you that your body is made of the different chemicals that were in the universe when this planet we live on, called Earth, was made out of the basic gases that existed at the dawn of time, and that it was the action of the energy from the sun on the gases that made life. Eventually, these people say, we developed out of the first tiny cells that were made then. They are scientists.

There are people who will tell you that a more important question than "Why am I alive?" is "What am I alive *for*?" and they spend all their time looking for reasons for humanity to exist. They are philosophers.

Some people think the answer to your question will be found in a mixture of religion, science, and philosophy. Others say that that's nonsense and it can only be found by believing in just one of those things. And yet others say that we won't know for centuries yet, if ever.

Maybe, when you grow up, you'll become one of the investigators who uncover clues to the answer to your question. I hope so, because I'd like to know too.

Dear Clare Rayner.

I was wondering if you could possibly answer this question. Do you know why I is am alive?

Richard

Dear Bushra,

I don't think you can say you love this boy, you know. You can't really love someone you don't know. It takes time and sharing a lot of things to be sure that love exists.

I think that you *fancy* this boy. He looks fun or he's good looking or he seems friendly and kind. Whatever it is, you'd like to get to know him better. And why not?

There are lots of ways to get to know him. One is just to walk up to him in school and say, "Hello." That may sound difficult but it isn't really. Imagine yourself doing that to someone you didn't fancy, but who you thought it would be nice to talk to. That will make it easier.

If you feel you can't do that, because you're shy, perhaps you can ask your Mum if you can have a few friends to play after school, say half a dozen. Then ask two girls and three boys and make this boy one of them. It will look friendly but not too "pushy".

Or, you could ask one of your girlfriends at school to arrange with her Mum for people to play in her house, and ask her to invite you and this boy too. *But make sure she's a good friend before you ask her to do this.* Some girls can be a bit unkind and tease someone they think fancies a person, and tell everyone else in school about it.

If you were to ask me the best one of these ways, I'd say the first one I suggested. If he's as nice as you think he is, he'll be friendly if you walk up and say, "Hello." If he isn't and treats you rudely or unkindly – well, you'll know that he isn't as nice as you thought, and you'll stop fancying him (not right away, but pretty soon!).

Good luck, Bushra!

Dear Clarier rayner

Their is a boy in my School
wha I love. He dosen't
knew. I have
no way of telling him
please could you help me
Please give me an answer.

Bushra

Dear Spanner,

You're quite right. It is not possible for people to live for ever. The stories you've seen on TV are just that – stories. People don't like the idea of not being alive, because most of us enjoy being alive so much. So they pretend to themselves that they will never die and make up stories about it. People have made up such stories ever since they discovered what death is and I expect they always will.

Mind you, there *is* a sort of way people live for ever – not in their own bodies, but in other people's memories. For example, I had a Grandma I loved a lot. I was very sad when she died, but after a while something interesting happened. The sad feelings went away, but what stayed inside my head and my feelings were the good things about her. She used to make me laugh, or said clever things that used to make me think. Now I am almost as old as she was when she died, but I still remember her and the funny clever things she said. So, in a way she is still living inside me, and she'll go on living as long as I am alive to remember her.

There are some very remarkable people who are remembered for even longer because they are so special that people tell their children about them, and they tell their children, and so on and on. People in history are like that – King Alfred who burned the cakes, or the first Queen Elizabeth. And of course people in religion are like that – Jesus Christ and Mohammed and Buddha.

So the answer to your question has to be no – and yes!

Dear Claire,

I would like to know if people can live forever. I have heard this on the telly and don't think it is true. Can this happen and has anyone ever done it?

Yours Sincerely
Spanner

Dear Sonia,

Little sisters can be very tiresome in such matters as who owns books and toys and pencils and so forth. The only answer has to be careful marking and protection of property.

What you need to do, as soon as you get something new, is mark it with your names. You can get sticky paper at any stationer's shop to write on so that it will stick to your things but not spoil them.

Then, if you can, find a way to keep your things put safely away, even locked up. Your own box with a key would be a useful thing to have. Maybe your Mum and Dad would see this as a good idea for one of your presents on your birthday or at Christmas? Then all you have to do is keep the key with you all the time.

I'm sure you're careful about not taking your little sister's things and using them. Sometimes older people think younger ones won't care – but they care about their property just as much as you do about yours. If you show that you too understand this and you treat each other's things the way you want your own treated, you'll find life will be a lot easier in your house.

FRY GUYS

Dear Clare Rayna,

my problem is that
I have two little sisters
& they keep taking mine
& my elder sisters propety.
Then they blame it on
us. Me & my sister are
worried we might get
scolded Please can you
help.

Yours
Sincerly
Sonia

Dear Syrene,

What you have to do is believe what your Mum told you!
She wants you to have a bike, obviously, but, like a lot of
people these days, she hasn't enough money to buy all
the things she'd like. Bikes cost a great deal – more than
enough to buy food for all your family for three weeks or
even longer (depending on how expensive a bike you
want!) and I'm sure you'll agree it's more important to
buy food for the family first than to buy your bike.

I dare say your Mum is saving as hard as she can to get
you what you want and the best way you can help her is
to stop asking. When you ask the same question over and
over instead of understanding the answer you've been
given, it's called nagging. And nagging doesn't help
mothers to save for bikes, because it makes them so
miserable.

So, the best thing you can do is wait as patiently as you
can till your Mum has finished her saving. It isn't easy for
you – but then neither is saving so hard easy for your
Mum!

Dear clairen,

My mum said that I chould have
a bike and she has not Brought
it me yet. I keep on asking
her but she says I will get you
it when I have money. I asked
her a few weeks ago and she said
No so what can I do? I dont
no what to do.

                    Yours   sincerely
                    Syrene

Bike

Dear Daine,

There are lots of differences between children and grown-ups. You don't only have a smooth face while your Dad has a beard. You also have a high voice while he has a deep one. You are short and he is tall. He has big muscles and yours are small. He has hair on his body and you haven't.

A time will come for you – when you are around eleven or so, or maybe a bit older – when the changes will start to convert you from a little boy into a man. You will grow bigger, stronger muscles. You will get taller. Your voice will swoop from being high to being gruff. And hair will start to grow on you where it never has before, on your chest and arms and legs and your belly and between your legs. And, of course, on your face.

Maybe you won't like the hair on your face, and will want to cut it off. A lot of men shave their faces every day. But there are men like your Dad who don't think this is necessary and like to keep the hair on their faces. They have to wash it and trim it just like the hair on their heads, of course, but it's worth the effort because it is so interesting. (Or so some people think. There are some who don't like to look at beards. I do, and I think you do.)

So in a way the answer to your question is very simple. Your beard is still inside you, waiting to grow.

Dear Claire Rayner
I was WONDERING,
IF You could answer
Why has My DaD
got a beard I am too
young
yours SINCerely,
Daine

Dear Sheetal,

There are a lot of things I can't do, either. I can't roller skate – I've tried so many times and I always fall over. I can't fly a kite – I've been trying to since I was your age.

There's a lot of things I can do, of course. I can swim and I can drive a car and I can cook. I couldn't when I was young, though. I had to learn how.

I'm telling you this to explain that some people can learn to do things as they get older and some never can. When you're at school you want to be able to do everything everybody else does, but as time goes by and you get older you discover that you just can't because nobody in the world can do everything. So you stop worrying about it. It would be nice if you could stop worrying now, though, wouldn't it? Then maybe you'd have a pleasant surprise. One day you'd have a try at riding your bike and because you weren't worried about it, you'd just somehow do it! It can happen that way.

As for worrying about growing – well, that really doesn't help at all. You can't make yourself grow. All you can do is eat your dinners and get lots of exercise running about and playing. Then you'll grow naturally to be the size you need to be. That's a promise.

PS As for not being able to sleep in the light – that's an easy one! Ask your Mum to get you a pair of eyeshades to put on at bedtime. They have them at the chemist's shop.

Dear Claire,
I cant fly my Kite
and I cant ride my bike
down the road and I
cant catch my boll
I cant grow and I cant
sleep in the night. I hope
you can help me
      Sheetal

Dear Deepa,

It takes some people a long time to learn how to be friends with more than one person at a time. It's very nice to have a lot of friends once you do know how. One day you can be with one of them and the next with a different one, while the first one also goes to someone else. It's all part of sharing with each other and having an interesting time hearing about each other's ideas and thoughts.

I wonder if the trouble is that your friend *has* learned this, but you haven't? Maybe when you think she isn't being your friend, she still is, but she happens to be with someone else at that moment.

Don't you like to talk to different people at different times? Maybe when you do some of your friends think you don't like *them* any more.

I think the best way to find out why your friend sometimes doesn't seem so friendly is to ask her. Choose a day when she is with you and *is* being your friend, and ask her what happens on the other days.

It really is the best way to find out for sure.

Dear clare Rayner,

This girl She
Sometimes
be's My friend
then she
dosn't

Your sinceely,
Deepa

Dear Darren,

Do you know something? I'm glad you find it difficult to make up your mind and reach decisions. It means that you're a thoughtful person and you don't just jump to conclusions. People who think they know enough about everything to make up their minds quickly worry me. It means they don't know how much they don't know. And they can do a lot of harm without meaning to.

But I can understand that sometimes it makes life hard for you if you can't make up your mind about things that don't matter too much. If your Mum says, "What do you want for supper? Sausages or hamburgers?" and you like them both, you need to decide soon, so that your Mum can get on with her cooking. So, how do you do it?

Maybe, sometimes, you can have the best of both worlds. For example, maybe your Mum will let you have a bit of each! However, if it's something like deciding whether to play in the swings park or go to the pictures, you can't do both. You have to choose.

You could try letting chance choose for you. Tossing a coin in the air and calling out, "Heads the park, tails the pictures," and then doing whatever the coin says is a way lots of people use.

Or, to be more scientific, you could try making lists. Write down one list of all the good things about, say, going to the park and then another of all the good things about going to the pictures. One list will certainly be longer than the other, and that will tell you what to do.

But don't be sorry you're the sort of thoughtful person you are. It's a good thing to be.

Dear clare Rayner,

This girl Sha
Sometimes
he's my friend
then she
dosn't

Your Sinceely,
Deepa

Dear Darren,

Do you know something? I'm glad you find it difficult to make up your mind and reach decisions. It means that you're a thoughtful person and you don't just jump to conclusions. People who think they know enough about everything to make up their minds quickly worry me. It means they don't know how much they don't know. And they can do a lot of harm without meaning to.

But I can understand that sometimes it makes life hard for you if you can't make up your mind about things that don't matter too much. If your Mum says, "What do you want for supper? Sausages or hamburgers?" and you like them both, you need to decide soon, so that your Mum can get on with her cooking. So, how do you do it?

Maybe, sometimes, you can have the best of both worlds. For example, maybe your Mum will let you have a bit of each! However, if it's something like deciding whether to play in the swings park or go to the pictures, you can't do both. You have to choose.

You could try letting chance choose for you. Tossing a coin in the air and calling out, "Heads the park, tails the pictures," and then doing whatever the coin says is a way lots of people use.

Or, to be more scientific, you could try making lists. Write down one list of all the good things about, say, going to the park and then another of all the good things about going to the pictures. One list will certainly be longer than the other, and that will tell you what to do.

But don't be sorry you're the sort of thoughtful person you are. It's a good thing to be.

Dear claire
              I am a boy aged 10
I like Swimming and runing
and drawing. why do I Find it
diFFicult to make up my
mind and reach decisions.

            yours Sincerely
                Darren

Dear Michelle,

The only person who can answer your question is your brother. Have you asked him?

Maybe he doesn't like piano music. Maybe he doesn't like your sort of piano music. Maybe he'd rather learn from someone else. There are lots of maybes. *And only he knows which one is the right one.*

So do ask him.

PS A lot of grown-ups don't think of asking the person who is giving them a problem just what it is that upsets them, so it's not a bit surprising that you never thought of it either. It's a pity people don't think of asking direct questions as soon as they have a problem with a person. It can sort things out so quickly when they do so. Try it – you'll see it works!

PPS Of course, when you ask your brother, you might not like the answer (he may say he doesn't like your music!). But that's a chance you have to take. At least you'll know.

Dear Clare Rayner,

        I was wondering Why does my brother shout at me when I'm teaching him the piano? Is it because my brother does not like lessons or because I play the piano all the time

Thankyou

<u>Yours sincerly</u>

Michelle

Dear Dill,

Oh, I do hope there'll never be another world war! I was a child, a little younger than you are now, when the last world war happened and it was *horrible*. I still remember all sorts of nasty things that happened. I don't think I'll ever forget, really.

And that's a good thing, because as long as there are some of us around who never forget how dreadful wars are, and who can teach other younger people about it all, the better the chances of there being peace.

I'm afraid that at present things in the world do look uneasy. People are fighting furiously in Bosnia. They are, too, in the Middle East and in other places around the world that we don't hear about so much. But we *do* have a system that is supposed to help people talk rather than fight – because "jaw jaw jaw is better than war war war" – called the United Nations. It is made up of all the countries in the world who wish to keep the peace. If we give them all the help we can to stop people fighting, it's possible we can stop another world war ever happening.

When you grow up, Dill, try to remember how much you hated thinking about war when you were the age you are now. Then, maybe, you'll become one of the good grown-ups who work at talking all the fighting away.

Dear Claire
    Do you think
there is going to
be a 3th World War
    Thankyou for
reading my letter

    Yours sinscerely
            DILL

Dear Peter,

There are two answers to your question.

The first is the personal one. You were born because your Dad and Mum loved each other a lot, so much that they wanted to be together all the time. So they got married. When people love each other so much they want to make love and making love is when a man puts one of his sperm inside the woman so that it can meet her egg. Then together they can grow into a baby. You.

But there is the not-so-personal answer, which is really about why anybody or anything is born. It's because of what some people call the Life Force and some people call Nature and other people call God. Whatever it is, we are all a part of life, and life, from the moment it first appeared on this planet, has shown one very strong need. *It likes being alive.* It wants to keep itself going for ever and ever and ever.

So, every individual piece of life, be it an earthworm or an apple tree, an eagle or your Mum and Dad, has this urgent feeling inside them to make new life. One day you'll get the same feeling and you'll find a girl to love and make love with, and make babies with. And then that baby will grow up and meet a partner and . . .

Well, I'm sure you can see what I mean.

I don't think that it matters what this is called, Nature or Life Force or anything else. I just think it's wonderful and I'm glad to be part of it. (It made me make three more human beings!) I hope you're glad too, because it's good to be alive, don't you think?

Dear claire
I am a boy I am ten
years old.

why are we Born?

I look forward to the
answer.

your sincerely
peter

Dear Anna,

All three of your questions really can be given one answer, which is – the world is not a fair place.

Some people are born to be clever and energetic and nice to look at. They find it much easier to earn money and get a home than people who are not clever and who can't work energetically, who are not as nice to look at.

Some people are born to families who want to have a baby to look after and who love that baby very much. Other people are born to families where no one has much time for them and not enough love. Those people who grow up in happy families are the ones who find it easiest to work and earn a living. Those who have a miserable time when they are little may grow up to be people who just can't work and earn properly and end up in the streets.

And because some of the fortunate people – the ones with good homes and cleverness and energy – don't understand the way life is for the others, they may bully them because they don't like them.

Or sometimes the unhappy ones look at the fortunate ones and hate them for having so much more than they have so they bully *them*.

So a lot of people have a lot, and a lot more have nothing. If only we could understand each other better and share out what there is more fairly it would be more comfortable, wouldn't it?

I'm glad you're concerned about these things. The world needs people like you who will grow up to try to make things better.

Dear, Claire,

Hi I am eleven Years old and I am
very quiet person. I have Two sisters one brother
and a mum. my mum has a boy friend called
Nicky and he is funny. I like him. I have a
pet dog called Brandy and my Birthday is in
November on the twenty-fifth. I got a lot of things
for Christmas and I enjoyed it.

I have some Quesions to ask you about a lot of
things. Here is quesion number one. Why do people
get bullied by other people?

2. why do some people get put out in the street?

3. why do people get less money than other people?
This is all for now I look forward to getting
your letter.

Your sincerely
Anna.

Dear Seema,

Isn't it horrible when people you trust let you down? I'm so sorry your ex-friend is threatening you like this.

I wonder what sort of secret it was you told her? Could it be one that maybe you could tell other people? A lot of other people? So many, in fact, that it wouldn't be a secret any more? Then it wouldn't matter what your ex-friend did or said, would it? She wouldn't be able to threaten you any more.

But if it's a real and important secret, then maybe you need a grown-up to help. If it is a family secret then tell someone in your family you feel comfortable with. Maybe your Mum or your Dad or your Grandma or someone like that. Then, they'll be able to help you not care if your nasty ex-friend tells tales.

If you can't talk to anyone at home, then you can definitely talk to a teacher at school about it. Not only your own teacher – you can ask any teacher you like to let you explain a problem to her (or him). Once you've got a grown-up to help you, you'll really feel much better.

In future, Seema, when you get over this crisis – and it will pass, truly it will – be very careful what you tell people, won't you? If it's a really important secret then keep it entirely to yourself. It's the only safe way.

Dear claire

I Have a problem. I have broken up with my friend. I told her a secret. I am worried about her telling everyone. Please Send me a letter as soon as possible.

your sincerely Seema

PLEASE before its too Late

Dear Rebecca,

There are two reasons why parents send their children to bed at a certain time. The first is because it is better for a child to get enough sleep. Do you know that it's while you're asleep that you do all your growing? You really do, so it's important for you to get enough sleep.

But there's another reason parents like earlier bedtimes than children do. They love their children very much and like to be with them, but they also love each other. When people love each other they like to be alone together sometimes. So, parents enjoy their quiet evenings after the children are in bed (though sometimes they also like to have their friends visit them, which is another reason to send you to bed earlier. Then they can concentrate on their friends. I'm sure you can understand that).

Maybe the best solution to your problem is to ask your parents to let you make a deal. Say you'll go to bed at their time if they let you read in bed or listen to the radio for a while before you turn out the light. That way you'll get the rest you need, they'll get the time to themselves they need and you'll all stop arguing.

PS By the way, tell your parents you're more likely to fall asleep if you're reading or radio-listening in bed than if you're just lying there thinking cross thoughts about early bedtimes.

Dear Clare Rayner

My Mum and Dad said
I have to go to
bed at 8:30 and
I don't Like to go
to bed at 8:30 What
Can I do.

Yours Faithfully
Rebecca

Dear Meg,

Congratulations on organising your club. It sounds like a very good one.

The main reason why people waste energy and make pollution is because they don't know any better.

It's only in the past few years that people have really started to think about such things as wasting energy. There has always been so much of it about you see. All the ancient sunlight stored underground in coal and oil seemed to be enough to last for ever and ever. But then, as people got healthier and healthier and lived longer and made more babies, the world got very full of people – too full, some think. The more people there are the more energy they use.

It's the same with pollution. People don't always know it's a bad thing to do. In a world without too many people the amount of waste and mess made was fairly easily cleaned up by Nature (she uses wind and water and bacteria and sunlight to do it) but in a crowded world it's much harder to get rid of it all. Especially when some of it comes from humanity's cleverness in using chemicals.

The answer is – well, more people like your club members, Meg. If you go about switching off lights when they aren't needed, make sure doors are kept closed in cold weather to keep heat inside and so on, and also are very careful about the things you use and the way you treat waste, you'll be teaching others to do the same. When enough people have learned, the problems will be solved. It will also help if people make sure they don't have too many babies, of course.

Dear Claire,

I am a girl aged 11 I have a club called "porlution breackers". I am the captain. There are 4 of us allogether, the members of my club are, Sian, Emma, donnet. I have a big family, My mum is a foster mum. I have no pets but I will Soon. I have a important question, Why do we Waste enegy and make more pollution. I look forward to hear from you.

Yours sincerely.

Meg.

Dear Samantha,

There are some quite good things about wearing school uniform. First of all, it means that you all feel as though you belong together. It's comforting sometimes to look about and realise that all the people are a sort of family. If you were out, say, and people from another school were picking on you, seeing some uniforms you recognised coming along the road would make you feel better.

It's also good because no one can show off. Some people at school will have rich parents and some won't. Not all rich parents are sensible. They might send their children to school dressed in such fancy clothes that those who couldn't afford them would feel miserable.

So I quite like the idea of uniforms, though parents often don't, because they cost more than ordinary clothes.

I agree with you about teachers though. I think they *should* wear something that shows they're teachers, while they're in school. Then if any unwanted strangers happened to come in, everyone would know it, wouldn't they? And it would help *them* feel like a family too.

The reason for having to ask to go to the lavatory – that's sensible too. Suppose people could wander off whenever they fancied and there was an emergency of some sort, even a fire, or it was important to find a person for some other reason? If you hadn't asked your teacher if you could go out of class, then no one would know where you were. And that wouldn't be a good idea at all.

Rules can seem silly, I know, but if you think of the reasons for them they seem quite sensible after all.

Dear Claire
I dont think its fear
at School
becouse we have to wear
school uniforms
and the teacher can wear
what thay like.
and we have to asked The Teacher
can we go to the tolit
do you think that right
          yours Sincerely
          Samantha

Dear Parsley,

I do like your name.

Your question is one scientists have been asking ever since the first dinosaur bones were discovered only a couple of hundred years ago, and still no one knows the answer for sure.

I can tell you they lived for millions and millions of years – a lot longer than we human beings have so far been in the world. So, they were very successful animals. I can also tell you there were lots of very different kinds, from the huge ones most people know about to quite tiny ones. They were a sort of reptile and some people think that their modern descendants are not only lizards, but also the birds.

Some people think they disappeared because the climate changed and got a lot colder. Others say it was the opposite – the climate got a lot warmer and the ice caps melted and the water rose and that's why they died – their home territories were flooded. Some say it was because they got so big they couldn't go on running, but I think that's not true, seeing that there were tiny ones as well as big ones. And some say it happened because meteorites – huge masses of stone – from outer space came and fell on our planet and changed the world.

The people who study dinosaurs and their bones are called paleontologists. If you are very interested in the subject you could get some good books from the library about it, and maybe grow up to become a paleontologist yourself. Because there are still lots of undiscovered dinosaurs. What do you think?

Dear claire

I am a Ten Year old Boy
and I live whith my mum
dad and sister. I was wondoring
if you could tell me why Did

Dinosaurs Become extinck. I Hope you
will be able to Help me
Yours sincerely

porshet

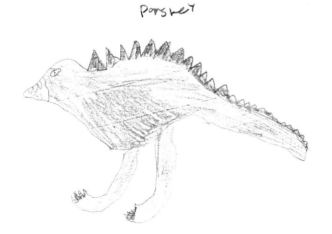

Dear Vinit,

One of the problems children have to deal with is the way grown-ups and children see the same things quite differently.

When you look at a Nintendo game, you see a brilliant game that would be a lot of fun and that you badly want.

When your Dad looks at one he sees something very expensive that won't last very long. He remembers things you may have forgotten, like other toys you wanted badly and when you got them, lost interest in quite soon. And your Dad doesn't like the idea of money being wasted.

Mind you, if you have the money saved out of your pocket money or presents, then maybe you can explain to him that since it's your money, you don't mind wasting it. He might listen to that. I wouldn't count on it, though.

One thing you can count on, I'm afraid; he's in charge of you and your life right now. When you're grown up you'll be able to spend your money any way you like, as long as you've earned it. By then you might be quite glad that your Dad taught you to be careful about it, because money is quite hard to come by, isn't it? Spending it carefully is a wise idea, if a bit on the dull side.

PS I do agree it's extra difficult if Mum says yes and Dad says no. I think you ought to ask them to talk to each other about this and make a definite decision one way or the other. To leave you dangling hopefully in the middle isn't very nice for you.

Dear Claire Rayner,

My name is Vinit, this is my question. My dad won't let me buy a Nintendo Game Boy. I have enough money is well. My mum says yes, but my dad says no. Can you please write back. Yours sincerely,

Vinit

Dear Katelin,

Being married is quite hard work. You have to look after
the person you are married to as well as yourself.
Husbands and wives have to worry about the person
they're married to, and share their worries. Most people
when they think of being married only think of the nice
bits, like cuddling a lot and sharing the good things, but
there are bad things that have to be shared too. It takes a
long time to learn how to do that. That's why it's better
for people to wait until they've done all their learning and
can take care of themselves before they get married and
have to take care of someone else as well.

There's something else. As you get older you learn
more and more about yourself, and your feelings, both
good and bad. You say you have a bad temper now. Well,
by the time you're old enough to think about marriage,
it's possible, even probable, that you'll have learned how
to deal with your temper sensibly, instead of just shouting
and stamping or whatever it is that you do now when
you're angry. If you were married now, though, and got
into one of your bad tempers, you'd be so horrid to be
with that the chances are that your husband wouldn't
want to stay with you. And then you'd be more angry and
upset than ever.

So it's worth waiting a while, don't you think?

Dear claire,

I some times have a bad temper. I like Art and rap songs.

Why can older people get married, and young people can not?

I hope you know the answer.

Yours sincerely,
katelin.

Dear Shawn,

I know the sky looks blue when you look up into it, but in fact it has no colour at all.

All round the earth there is a layer of air – if there wasn't we wouldn't be here. It's air that keeps us going. That air is made up of millions and billions and trillions of atoms of gases and unbelievably tiny drops of water and parts of chemicals and all sorts of things like that.

Above the layer of air there is space and space is black.

When the rays of the sun shine through space and into our air, they make light so that we can see, and that light reflects from some of the tiny parts in the air – especially the water drops – so that we get the light from them as well as directly from the sun. At the same time the seas and earth below the air, where we are standing, also reflect the light and send it upwards. So, when we look up into the sky we see light reflections – and because the darkness of space is shining through the reflections that makes us see the colour blue. In places where the sea is very blue, like the Mediterranean, the sky will look even more blue and in places where the sea is quite grey looking, like the North Sea, the sky looks less blue. And if you fly very high in a plane, and go nearer the edge of the air shield round the earth (called the atmosphere) the sky looks a much darker blue. So the sky and sea are both mirrors showing each other reflections of themselves.

You can find out more about the atmosphere and the way sun and light behave by reading good books about science. Your library will have some good ones, with lots of pictures. Do ask the librarian to help you find some.

Dear claire

Why is the sky blue.

I hope that you had a
nice christmas and all
the best for 1993

your sincerely
Shawn

Dear Peter,

I know it would be easier for all of us if we all spoke the same language. It would mean we could really talk properly to each other instead of misunderstanding because we don't recognise each other's words. Maybe with one language we would stop having wars. There are people who think this, and they tried to invent a language everyone could speak, and called it Esperanto, but it isn't very popular, because mostly people prefer to speak the language they learned when they first started to talk – their mother tongue, it's called.

The reason there are so many languages is that when humanity first appeared, it wasn't in just one place. We started to bob up in many different places. We developed from the apes and the chimpanzees (most people agree nowadays this is what happened – that we evolved from the higher apes) and we learned to use our throats and our tongues and our voice boxes to make noises to communicate with each other. Slowly those noises were made into recognisable sounds, which we now call words. Naturally, the people who lived in a valley in Africa, say, invented different words from the people who started in the middle of America. Each set started their own language.

But there is a very surprising thing. Human languages, however different they are from each other, have some matching things. We all use words which are names of things and words which are doing words (called verbs) and we all make sentences, though the different parts of them may be in different orders. So the ability to use language is something we're born with. Isn't that useful?

Dear Claire

I am 11 years old.
I live in a family of 5.
I have a brother and a
sister. My question is why
do we speak different languages

Yours sincerely

Peter.

Dear Diana,

I am sorry that you're so unhappy. It's very hard for a child to be happy when her Mum and Dad are having arguments a lot. And it's particularly hard when the child has to be part of the arguments.

Are you part of them in your house? Do your Mum and Dad talk to you separately about their arguments? If they do it might be easier if you tell them both you don't like that. It's like asking you to take sides. Ask them to talk to you together. Then you'll find it easier to understand what each of them is upset about.

You say that the problem is that your Dad wastes money. Money can upset people a lot, I know. If your Dad won't listen to your mum when she asks him not to be wasteful and if he won't listen to you (and have you told him how upset you are? If not, why not try?) then is there anyone else who can talk to him? Maybe your Grandma – the one who is your Dad's Mum – would be a good person. Or maybe your Dad has a brother or a sister – your uncle or aunt – who could help.

Certainly it's too much of a problem for you to deal with. You can't make your Dad stop wasting money and you can't make him stop ignoring the bills. But maybe, with help, you can get him to understand why everyone gets so unhappy when he does these things. And that might help him to decide to change himself. Because he is the only one who can do it, I'm afraid. No one else can.

I'm truly sad for you. I'm sure when you grow up you'll choose a husband who is sensible about money, now you know how much sadness not being sensible can cause.

Why are my parents always
fighting over bills My dad Wastes
a lot of money While My MuM Works
I want My dad to do Something good.
and My dad to Make More Money
So My dad Could pay all the bills.
And be a happy family

please Write back

From Diana

Dear Cori,

I'm glad you're out of plaster now and rid of your crutches. I hope you don't break any more bones.

I have to be boring about answering your question about being in love and tell you that there isn't an easy answer. It's one of those things you just know about and to tell the truth, if you have to ask "How do you know you're in love?" it means you never have been. One day you will be and, oh boy, but you'll know it then!

As for dying – well, there are some people who believe there is a heaven and a hell. A great many more do not. I am one of these. I believe that we are like all other life on this planet – made of chemicals and water and other materials (there are lots of library books where you can find out the details) and when we die and are put in the earth we gradually become those substances again. The substances are taken up by plants as food, and then animals eat the plants and people eat both the plants and the animals, so that all the materials we're made of once belonged to someone else, and when we die they'll go on to become yet another person. So, though no one lives for ever, we all sort of do, don't we?

I hope you like this answer. I find a lot of children *do* like to know that nothing in this world is wasted and we are each part of all people in this interesting way.

My regards to your four best buddies.

PS Ask your teacher about an old song called "On Ilkla' Moor". It's all about what happens when people die.

Dear Claire,

Hi I am a bad Person but Can be good. I Sometimes get on weel weel with others and i have 4 very best buddies. I am eleven i had my birthday right after Chrintmas. Oh and by the way I'm a boy. A couple of months ago i broke my knee Cap. I was in plaster and was on Crutches for over 8 weekes.

I have at least 2 questions to ask and here they are. My first one is this. How do you know When you are in love? My Second questoin is What happens when you die? They Say that good people go to heaven and bad go to hell. Is this true?

yours Sincerely
Cori

Dear Amy,

You have made a great discovery. You have spotted one of the two things which make us different from animals.

One is speech. We can make words and make other people understand what we mean and what we want. When you say to people, "Please give me that apple," they know at once what you want. Animals can't do that.

And the other special thing is our thumbs. They are called opposable thumbs because they can be arranged to be opposite to our fingers. And that makes us just about the cleverest creatures there are. Bees build hives, ants build nests, beavers cut down trees and moles dig tunnels, but because we have a pair of opposable thumbs, we can do all these things and more.

Because we can pick things up and hold them. If we didn't have thumbs we could never have picked up stones or sticks when we first became people, millions of years ago. If you want to know how hard it is to pick things up without a thumb, watch a cat trying to hook a fish out of water, or a dog trying to get bits off a bone. They have to use their teeth, their noses, and their paws all curved and awkward. We just bend our thumbs and there you are!

This is why we became tool makers. Why we built ourselves houses. Why we made equipment for farming. Why we made everything humans do make – most of them wonderfully good, and some of them bad, like bombs. Our thumbs, together with our speech, made it all possible because once you can talk you can pass on knowledge and become very special and clever people.

So, let's cheer for thumbs; they're wonderful!

Dear Clare Rayner

Please will you
answer this question for me. If you
could this is it.
Why do we have a thumb going
the opposite way to our fingers?

Yours sincerely
Amy

Dear Laura,

I do wish I could meet you. You must look very interesting with your rainbow-coloured hair.

You've asked one of the hardest questions there is.

People are made by Nature to fall in love with each other, so that new people can be made. Nature only wants one thing, really – lots and lots of new life. Falling in love with someone when you're old enough to make babies makes you want to make love with them, which is how babies are made.

Why do people fall in love with the people they fall in love with? I expect that was what you really wanted to know most.

It's impossible to know why one person sees another and immediately feels all soppy and excited inside, which is the first stage of falling in love. Maybe the person they see looks like someone else they've always loved, like their Mum and Dad. If you look at happy couples, you may see that often they do look a bit like each other's parents. Try looking at your family photos sometime and see if that is what happened in your family.

Sometimes people fall in love with the first person who comes along at a time when they're feeling good and they want someone to share their happiness with them.

Sometimes people look for someone to fall in love with, just because all their friends are doing it (this is really a pretend falling-in-love).

These are a few of the very very many reasons why people fall in love. I dare say you'll meet some people who'll give you a lot of different answers.

Dear Claire

People have told me about you and I keep saying to my-self that I will meet you and I'm going to tell you about me. My name is laura. I'm 10 years old and I have brown and pink and orange hair because. my mum dyed it for fun. My hair is down to my shoulders and curley. My eyes are brown.

Please can you tell me why people fall in love?

Thank you for reading my letter, claire

Yours sincerely.
laura.

Dear Amy,

You've answered your own question, you know! Yes, one of the reasons some boys are bullies is that they have been bullied or picked on themselves. People learn from what they see and what happens to them, don't they? If you live in a family where everyone is polite and kind to each other, then you grow up thinking it's the right way to be and when you start school, then you treat the people you meet there in the way you've been treated. But if you've been hit a lot and been picked on, then of course you'll treat the people you meet in *that* way.

You ask about whether it's in boys' natures to be bullies and some people say it is. There are grown-ups who will tell you that boys and men are born to be selfish and unkind. Other grown-ups (and I am one of them) definitely don't think so. We think that while it's true that boys can be noisy sometimes and bouncier and more interested in throwing things and bashing about than girls, it's not true of all boys. Just as it isn't true that all girls are gentle and nice and kind, which is what some people think. I've met girls who are unkind and spiteful and who hit others smaller than themselves.

And, of course, so have you! That's why you ask why girls are nasty to each other sometimes. And it's for the same reasons boys are.

But I do believe people can *learn* to be kind and polite, even if they don't feel particularly friendly. I hope you do that, because when you do you're helping to teach people to be nicer to get on with. I expect you do, actually, and that's why you asked your question.

Dear claire

Why do you think boys in are
School and some more schools are bullys
do you think its because. I have been
bullyed or picked on or do you think
its dust in there nature? and Why do
you think girls be nasty to each other.
Some girls get on nice but others can
be so so nasty. Why cant people
Stay Friends. Thank you For your
time.

yours   Sincerely
                    AMY

Dear Claire
       I am a Boy
and I am 18 yeres old

Why do I get bad dreams
aboutt my granddad ~~the~~ died
when I was born.

       Yours sincerely
       Wally

Dear Wally,

I'm sorry to hear you have bad dreams. They're horrid, aren't they? They make you feeling tired and sad all day.

There are lots of reasons for having bad dreams, but for children the most likely is not being told enough of the truth about things. Grown-ups often think that if they don't talk to children about difficult subjects, then the children will never think about them, and will have no problems. That's not true, of course. Children think a lot about things even if grown-ups don't mention them. But most grown-ups have forgotten this even though they were children themselves.

Death upsets grown-ups a lot. Well, no one would pretend that the thought of dying is a nice one. Most of us enjoy being alive very much and don't want to think it will ever stop. But of course it will, one day. Everything that lives has to die eventually, to make space for all the new lives that keep coming along.

Perhaps no one in your family or any of the grown-ups you know have ever learned to be comfortable about this fact. Perhaps that is why they don't talk to you sensibly about death and dying. Maybe, they even whisper about it if you're around and that makes you feel frightened. Or maybe they cry about it and then won't tell you why they're crying. All of this can make you feel very bad. If your Granddad is the person in your family who died most recently then that will be the dead person you'll worry about most, even though you never knew him. All of this adds up to making bad dreams for you.

The answer is to talk to someone about death and dying, someone who can help you understand how natural it is, and how there is no need to be so frightened all the time.

If there is no one in your family who is easy to talk to, ask your teacher at school. I'm sure she'll help you a lot. Once you've done all the talking you need, you'll be able to think proudly and with interest about the many ancestors you had, including your Granddad, and you won't be afraid any more. The bad dreams will stop. That's a promise.

Dear Sivachelvi,

How kind of you to be my best friend. I appreciate that.

I'm sorry people tease you. I can think of three reasons why. The first may surprise you. It's because they like you. They think you're nice and it's a strange thing but people sometimes feel embarrassed about liking others. So they pretend not to and tease to hide their feelings.

People also tease because it makes them feel strong and clever when they aren't. If you can make someone go red and feel squirmy inside, just by saying silly things, it makes you feel good.

The third reason is copy-catting. If one person teases you, others who are shy and want to be friends with the teaser copy him, just to make him like them. Then, when other shy people see there are two teasers at work, they get the same idea, and join in.

The cure for the teasing depends on why it's being done. If it's because people like you, then just smile and laugh when it happens and soon they'll feel more comfortable about liking you.

If it's being done to make the teaser feel strong and clever – well, don't show you've been hurt. Don't squirm and don't cry. Instead put on a show. Smile and laugh. The teaser won't be able to feel strong and clever then.

If it's being done by copy-catters then you have to stop the person who started it all. Then the copy-catters will stop too. And the best way? Yes. Just smile and laugh.

Not only does it help stop a lot of the teasing when you pretend not to care – you actually *do* stop caring.

Do try it, and I'll bet you it works.

Dear Claire,
                    not
        I don't think it's a fear
because everybody teses me I feel
very un-happy when they teses me
Please tell me what can I can do

     Your
        Best Friend
                  SIVACHELVI

Dear Katharine,

Sharing a mother and father is quite difficult, so is sharing a house. Most of us don't like having to wait, or to do without. But if you share a Mum and a Dad and perhaps a bedroom and bathroom, sometimes obviously you can't have what you want when you want it.

So, if your Mum is busy with you when your sister wants something, that will make your sister angry. She'd probably like to hit your Mum because she gets cross with her for being busy with you, but most children worry about hitting their Mums. It's easier to hit someone else and you're the next best person for your sister to hit when she's cross. You're nearer her size, for a start, and secondly she won't be so worried about hitting you.

The same thing happens if she wants the bathroom and you're in it, or she wants to make your bedroom or playroom tidy and you don't (or the other way round!). She gets angry and hits you.

Now, you don't say whether *you* ever hit *her*, but I'm going to guess that you do sometimes. I guess that because when I was your age and had sisters and brothers we hit each other a lot. When I was a mother with three little children they hit each other a bit, too, sometimes.

But there wasn't too much hitting by my three little children because we – their Mum and Dad – remembered how much we didn't like it when we were young, so we tried to find ways to help our children share us and their house without getting too angry. Have you asked your Mum and Dad to help you and your sister this way? It can be very useful.

Dear Clare Rayner

I was wondering? Why? my? sister keeps? on? hitting? me.

yours Sincerely
Katharine

Dear Michael,

Did you know there are more than 5¼ billion people in the world and *every one* is different? Some look like their mothers and fathers and some look like their brothers and sisters, but all of them are unique. That's true even of twins who may look the same but aren't.

That's because when new people are made they are made by mixing the egg cells of mothers with the egg cells of fathers – and those cells are themselves already a mixture, because each mother has cells which are a mixture of *her* mother and father and each father has cells which are a mixture of *his* father and mother. And of course, each of the fathers and mothers, as far back as you can go, were mixtures of their fathers and mothers . . .

What this means is that you, Michael, are not just a half of each of your Mum and your Dad, but also a quarter of each of your grandparents, and an eighth of your great-grandparents and so on, way back into the past.

Each one of these great-grandparents and each one of those that came before and after them have passed something on to you – perhaps the shape of your head or the size of your nose or the sort of personality you have. And of course the colour of your eyes. Some of your ancestors had those blue eyes your Mum and brother have and some the brown eyes you and your Dad have.

When you grow up and make babies, they may have blue or brown eyes. If the mother of your babies has hazel eyes, or green ones, or grey ones, your babies may inherit their eye colour from her, so they'll be unique too. Just like you.

Dear Clare
I was wondering

wy do me and my Dad
have bumh eyes
and my mum and my
bapther have Blue
thahk your
michael

Dear Charlotte,

But we do come out of eggs! Not exactly as birds do, but still, it's quite similar.

When birds want to make new babies, they mate. The mother bird makes tiny eggs inside her body and so does the father bird – only his eggs are called sperm. When they mate – it's called making love – the father bird puts sperm inside the mother bird and the two sorts of egg join together, so that each baby is made half of its mother and half of its father. Inside the mother the egg starts to grow.

After a while it grows a hard shell and the mother bird then pushes the egg out of her body and settles it in a warm soft nest. There the baby bird goes on growing while the mother bird sits on the egg to keep it warm.

When the baby is so big it fills the whole shell, it breaks a hole with its beak and comes out all wobbly, but able to walk a bit, and ready to finish growing in the world outside.

Well the same sort of thing happens with people. A mother and a father who want to make a baby also grow eggs and sperm. Then the father puts his sperm inside the mother so that it can meet her egg. The two join together to make a baby who is half her mother and half her father. The egg starts to grow like the bird's egg does.

But now it gets different. Instead of putting a hard shell round her egg and pushing it out into a warm soft nest outside her body, a human mother settles her eggs in a soft warm nest *inside* her body. (The nest is called her uterus, by the way. Or sometimes it's called her womb. It's interesting, isn't it, how many different words people have for the same thing?)

Anyway, there the egg grows and grows and grows and turns into a baby. And when she's big enough to breathe and eat by herself, though not yet able to walk about or talk or anything, her mother pushes her out of her body to go on growing as a separate person. So you see, birds and people are a bit the same, as well as being a lot different.

There's one difference between birds and people most of us are quite pleased about. Human mothers make milk in their bodies to feed their babies after they're born. They make it in their breasts and the baby sucks them to get food. Birds don't make milk. They go and get worms and flies and slugs and snails to give to their babies.

I'm very glad I'm a person and not a bird, when it comes to food, aren't you, Charlotte?

Dear Claire

I am 11 years old short. I have blue eyes and brown hair I have many friends In a middle of a lesson I get told off.

Why do we have rules
Why do foreigners speak different to us.

I hope you can write back.
yours sincerly
Russell.

Dear Russell,

We have rules because we – most people, that is – like to live in big groups. There are some animals on this planet (and we're a sort of animal too, after all!) which like to be by themselves all the time. Certain kinds of big cats – tigers, for example – are like that, and only meet each other when they want to mate and make babies. Otherwise, they walk alone.

But we love a crowd. We like to be part of a family, of a neighbourhood, of a district, of a city, of a country, of a continent and so on. People like to say proudly, "I'm English!" or "I'm French!" or whatever they are. It makes them feel safe and comfortable to belong to the crowd that is theirs.

That is the good news. The bad news is that if a lot of people live together they can get into terrible fights unless there are ways to stop them. We all like to have our own way to do what we want to do when we want to do it. (Well, I know I do, and I've never yet met anyone who wasn't just the same. So I expect you are too.)

The only way to make sure there are as few fights as possible is to make a set of rules that everyone agrees are good ones. Sometimes the rules are made by religion. The Ten Commandments are a set of religious rules that are very sensible living rules. If you don't steal from people or interfere in their marriages or kill them, or tell lies, then it's much harder for there to be fights, isn't it? Every group of people in the world has rules like these. They're called laws, which is just another name for rules.

Most rules are very sensible, like everyone driving on the same side of the road. Imagine the crashes if they could drive where they fancied! In some countries the rules are cruel, so that people suffer. So there are people trying to make sure that there are laws for the whole world to protect all the people in it.

It isn't easy to make good rules, but we certainly need them.

First published in Great Britain in 1993 by
Kyle Cathie Limited
7/8 Hatherley Street, London SW1P 2QT

ISBN 1 85626 112 3

Claire Rayner is hereby identified as the author of this
work in accordance with Section 77 of the Copyright,
Designs and Patents Act 1988.

A Cataloguing in Publication record for this title is
available from the British Library.

Designed by Geoff Hayes
Printed in Belgium by Proost